I Am Not Afraid

Copyright © 1986 Concordia Publishing House
3558 S. Jefferson Avenue, St. Louis, MO 63118-3968
Manufactured in the United States of America

All rights reserved. No part of this publication may be reproduced, stored in a retrieval system, or transmitted, in any form or by any means, electronic, mechanical, photocopying, recording, or otherwise, without the prior written permission of Concordia Publishing House.

Library of Congress Cataloging-in-Publication Data

Jones, Rebecca, C.

    (Self-concept book)
    Summary: A child overcomes fear of such things as the dark, a big dog, and thunder and lightning, through an awareness of the presence of Jesus.
    1. Fear—Religious aspects—Christianity—Juvenile literature. 2. Children—Religious life. [1. Fear. 2. Christian life] I. Mattozzi, Patricia, ill. II. Title. III. Series.
BV4571.2J66   1986   248.8'2   86-984
ISBN 0-570-09113-6

---

3 4 5 6 7 8 9 10 11   03 02 01 00 99 98 97 96 95

I am not afraid.

I am not afraid
of the dark . . .

until night.

I am not afraid of falling . . .

until I'm at the top of the monkey bars, and there's no way down.

I am not afraid
of bumble bees . . .

until one buzzes by
with his stinger hanging out.

I am not afraid
of the big dog next door that barks . . .

until he comes outside
with his mouth wide open,
and I can see his sharp teeth.

I am not afraid
of the new baby-sitter . . .

until my mother leaves,
and it looks like she's never coming back.

I am not afraid of snakes . . .

until I think I see one
slithering in the grass.

I am not afraid
of lightning and thunder . . .

**until they flash
and boom across the sky.**

I am not afraid
of the spiders
that crawl in the basement . . .

until I have to go down there.

I am not afraid
of monsters
or burglars or kidnappers . . .

until I hear a noise in the hall.

Sometimes, when it's night,
  or I climb to the top of the monkey bars,
  or a bee buzzes by,
    or the big dog comes out,
      or my mother leaves,
        or I see a snake,
          or lightning flashes across the sky,
            or a spider comes crawling at me,
            or there's a noise in the hall . . .

                    sometimes I am *very* afraid.

But then I remember
that Jesus is my Friend
and He is always with me.
And, then, I am not
so afraid after all.